I0541908

Making
A
Difference

Making
A
Difference

A Country Girl's View
—Take Two

KELLIE KUNZLER

JK

BAR JK PUBLISHING

Making A Difference: A Country Girl's View – Take Two
Copyright © 2024 by Kellie Kunzler
All rights reserved, including the right to reproduce
distribute, or transmit in any form or by any means.
Except as permitted under the U.S. Copyright Act of 1976, no part of this book
may be reproduced, distributed, or transmitted in any form or by any means,
or stored in a database or retrieval system without the written permission of the
authors, except in the case of brief passages embodied in critical reviews and
articles where the title, author and ISBN accompany such review or article.

For information contact:
kelliekunzlerauthor@gmail.com
www.kelliekunzlerauthor.com
Facebook/KellieKunzlerAuthor

Published by:
Bar JK Publishing

Copy Editor: Kim Autrey • Content Editor: Debbie Ihler Rasmussen
Cover design by difrats • Cover photo by sailorsoul
Interior book design by Francine Platt, Eden Graphics, Inc.
Photo on title page by Cherilyn Kunzler

Hardcover   979-8-89454-025-2
Paperback   979-8-89454-024-5
eBook   979-8-89454-026-9
Audio   979-8-89454-027-6

Library of Congress Control Number: 2024920607

Manufactured in the United States of America

DEDICATION—TAKE TWO

To my dad

For the short time you were here,
you made a difference.

All these years later,
you still continue to inspire me.

JK

Dear Reader,

WHEN I STARTED putting this book together, I discovered a theme among this collection of my writings. It was about people who made a difference in the lives of someone else. And it was nice to look back at people and things that inspired me.

We might never truly know how much we made a difference to someone else. But I want you, Dear Reader, to know that you have made a difference in my life.

I hope you find some inspiration within these pages. But most of all, I hope you are able to feel God's love for you.

Kellie Kunzler

JK

Anyway

THERE IS A QUESTION I've asked myself many times.

Why do I even try?

I still don't know what the answer is. But, it might have something to do with not giving up hope of somehow making a difference.

I'm the first one to admit I don't have a green thumb. I wish I did. I really admire those people who can grow anything and see it survive and thrive. I have the desire, just not the touch.

My kids will tell you any plant I touch is sure to die. Well, that's not true. Three years ago on Mother's Day, my youngest daughter, Hope, gave me a couple of succulent plants. They are sitting proudly in my kitchen window alongside a geranium plant a friend gave me. They look a little haggard, but they are alive.

But if we are keeping score, I've lost more plants than I want to admit. I planted a bunch of trees when we moved into our current house. Out of the thirty I've planted over the years, two are still alive. I'll call it a win. Maybe one day, even here in the desert, I will have a beautiful yard. (I hope.)

I've always liked this quote: *Do it anyway*. I always thought it was from Mother Teresa. But I learned Mother Teresa actually quoted those thoughts from Kent M. Keith's poem, "Paradoxical Commandments."

That saying has stuck in my mind, and I've pondered it over and over. If people treat you mean, be kind anyway. If you work hard building something and it gets destroyed, build it anyway (including your yard).

Many times, we tend to talk ourselves out of doing things. "What's the point?" Other times we may listen to those voices that tell us it's too hard or a waste of our time. But you know what? You may never be a Rembrandt or

Charles M. Russell. But, if you want to paint something, do it anyway. So what if you make mistakes while playing the piano or any other instrument? I make mistakes on the organ every Sunday. Keep playing anyway. Your music or art can touch the hearts of those around you, including your own.

I have a very special picture sitting on my dresser. It's a watercolor of the schoolhouse that I attended as a child. It was a card painted by Barbara, a special lady I knew while growing up, so I framed it. She was given a few opportunities to do big projects, but mostly she shared that talent with friends and neighbors. One of her paintings of a beautiful landscape hung on the wall of my childhood home. After my mom died, I kept it. Every time I look at it, it reminds me of that special lady, her talent, and kindness.

Barbara made a difference in people's lives because she chose to share her talent. She didn't become rich and famous, but she chose to paint anyway. And I'm so grateful she did.

Based on my many years of experience in

starting projects, and quitting. Teaching piano, and students quitting. I'm pretty sure you have probably started to learn something, then got discouraged and quit. We lose interest, or we talk ourselves out of finishing something. Usually, because we feel that we'll never be good enough at it, or we're just bored.

Guilty again.

Sometimes we put effort and time into creating something, only to have it be destroyed. It can feel like we wasted time, energy, and resources, and have nothing to show for it. This might be a good time to turn to God and seek His guidance.

When we pray, God will answer our prayers. It may not be what we were expecting, or make any sense, but we can choose to hold on to our faith anyway. Keep praying.

Will our actions really make a difference in the overall picture? I believe they will.

We can make the world a better place when we make the choice to be kind anyway, forgive anyway, do good anyway, or create anyway.

Another quote Mother Teresa often referred

to is, "In the end, it is between you and God. It was never between you and them anyway."

That says it all.

JK

A Good Story

I LOVE A GOOD STORY.
I love it even more when it's a true story.

One of my favorite things to do is read about my ancestors. Well, not just mine. I can get lost down the *rabbit hole* looking up other people on genealogy websites.

In fact, as I'm writing this, I have been side-tracked into a maze of different life stories as I've been looking through my family line.

Through reading and sharing life experiences, we can feel a connection to our family.

When my great-great-grandmother Nancy was sixteen, she became ill. Her legs became crippled as a result of the medicine she was treated with. But this did not prevent her from accomplishing many things. Four years later, she and her fiancé, Joseph, had set the wedding date for January 1. He braved the cold, swollen river to marry her. Although the condition of the river was a major obstacle, he was a man who kept his promises. He fastened his trunk to the buckboard, hitched his grey mares to it, and climbed in the seat. He drove to the edge of the riverbank, spoke to his team, and they plunged into the swollen river and swam safely across. Nancy and Joseph were married January 1, 1847, in Ohio. They eventually moved out West and raised a family. Nancy would scoot around her home in a chair to do her daily tasks, and her hands were always busy. Joseph and Nancy had a good life together.

What a great example of determination, commitment, and perseverance. When I first read Nancy's story, I felt an immediate connection and compassion for her. As someone who has struggled all my life with leg, ankle, and feet issues, I could relate to Nancy. I've read her diary she wrote later in her life. She didn't travel much, but she was constantly busy. I'm so glad someone was able to share that about her.

Another favorite story is about my grand-parents. They lived just a little over three miles away from my grandmother's parents in the small Almo Valley in Southern Idaho. Long before there were telephones, they would use a mirror to talk with each other. There were times my grandfather wasn't home, and if Grandma had troubles, she would flash the mirror, and someone would come to help.

Using a mirror to send signals to communi-cate sounds cool. Especially when you realize the only other alternative was to walk or saddle up a horse or hook up the wagon and travel however many miles to visit with someone. I'm old enough to remember a time before every-one had a cell phone. I feel blessed to be able to talk with my family and friends often with-out leaving my home. I honestly didn't think I'd ever live to see video calls being used every day by ordinary people. I'm very grateful I have that technology available to me today.

A few years ago, my sisters and I spent a summer day getting to know our four cousins who we are related to on our mother's side. I have memories of visiting their parents' home with my mom when I was a little girl. These four sisters are amazing, strong women. We each shared the story of our lives and how we ended up where we were.

And even though we knew many of the same stories about our ancestors, we each had a story or two from family records that the rest of us hadn't heard before. It was fun to share them with each other.

This is one of my cherished memories because shortly after that visit, one of the cousins lost her battle with cancer. I'm so grateful we took the time to connect, and my sisters and I still stay in touch with the other three. Our lives have been enriched by getting to know them better.

Not everyone is blessed to know their ancestors. For some people, that might even be a good thing. But we can learn so much about who we are when we can read their stories. That's why it is so important for us to write things down or find another way to record our life story.

I have struggled over the years to keep a journal. But one thing that made a big impression on me as a child was looking at the calendar and seeing what was scheduled for our family. We had a family country/western dance band, so I was mainly interested in where and when we were scheduled to play for a dance. So, for years, that's what I did for journaling.

I kept track on a calendar when we moved the cows, the price we sold them for, when we cut the hay, trips to town, the county fair, birthdays, and other important events. I have a stack of old calendars that I can't part with because they hold a record of my family's life.

One of the assignments for my genealogical writing class was a three-generational history. I decided to write about myself, my mother, and my grandmother. Both my mom and her mom have passed away. It was a good way to make a record of their lives so future generations could know a little bit about them. One of these days I want to extend that history back even further to my great-grandmother.

When one of my daughters realized that I

was writing some of my life story down, she told me, "Good, now we'll know what to put in your obituary." I had to laugh. *Glad I could be of help.*

In the autobiography of one of my favorite authors, he talks about his sister telling him what she was going to say about him at his funeral. He realized he didn't want to be known for the things she chose to focus on. That inspired him to write his own life story and include the stories and experiences that were important to him.

Do you ever wonder what will be said to describe your life when you're no longer around? Something to think about.

I treasure the things that my ancestors personally wrote down about their lives.

I am also eternally grateful for those who took the time to write about the events that are recorded in the Scriptures. The example set by Jesus, His words, and the messages of love and hope while overcoming trials have affected mankind for centuries. Each account shared may have a different viewpoint, but the overall message is the same.

So, the next time your sister, or aunt, or whoever asks you to write down what you've been doing for the last few years so she can add it to the family scrapbook, do it. When I graduated with my degree in Family History Research, my family celebrated by going out to dinner and surprising me with a binder containing their personal histories. These are the same kids who still give me short answers when I ask them how their day was and complain if I want details. I recognize the effort it took for them to write their stories. It made their gift to me just that more special.

Genealogy isn't just a hobby for old people. There are histories and stories rich with wisdom for all generations. And if you find yourself getting lost down the *rabbit hole*, never fear. If you keep going, it just might lead you *home*.

JK

Deep Roots

HERE ARE MANY CEDAR TREES on our property. But there is one that has always been special to me. It stands close to some corrals, right in the path of where we turn the canyon water. I am amazed by this tree. Its tenacity to survive inspires me.

Each spring as the snow melts in the mountains, the water flows freely down the canyon, and we irrigate our fields and meadows. But when the canyon water dries up, the only water those trees get is rain, which is pretty scarce most summers.

The roots on this special tree protrude before disappearing under the ground. The soil here isn't the best and it's rocky, so I've often wondered just how deep they go.

In spite of everything against it, that cedar continues to stand tall and immovable. And many creatures seek shelter and shade under its branches.

Life gets hard sometimes. When I wonder how to hold on and keep the faith that things will be all right, I think of this tree. It's not like the other cedar trees around our ranch. It's shaped different, and its roots are showing. Actually, that is part of why I like it so much. And I assume its roots run pretty deep and are very strong. I'm reminded to check how deep my roots are in my faith in God.

How deep are *your* roots?

I have some pretty funny (and frustrating) stories about trucks backing into cedar trees around our ranch. My father-in-law was notorious for backing up a truck, usually the one-ton flatbed, until he hit something, usually a tree, then moving forward without worrying about the damage he left behind. The most notorious story is when he backed into a neighbor's small shed and knocked it off the foundation. Then

he drove off without realizing what he had done. Thankfully they didn't hold it against him. But our family could write an entire book of just Dee stories. Let's just say that the *backing up* gene is alive and well with my family.

The point I want to make in sharing those funny stories is that, even with the punishment inflicted on them, the trees have all survived. Some may show a little wear; especially the one tree that stands next to Henry's chicken coop, because it's been hit multiple times. But, if your roots run deep, you can survive almost anything.

May *your* roots go deep enough that when you are hit with adversity and trials, or a truck—well hopefully not a truck—you are still able to stand strong and your faith be unmoved.

Snapshot

THERE IS AN IMAGE in my mind of a special moment in my life.

My husband needed to irrigate the field behind our house. He grabbed the shovel, rested it on his shoulder, climbed over the wire fence, and started walking along the ditch through the growing alfalfa crop. He wore his worn western shirt, faded Wranglers, beat-up straw cowboy hat, and irrigating boots.

Five-year-old Will was determined to go help and had grabbed his plastic shovel, climbed through the fence, and was following his dad. He was wearing similar attire, including a beat-up straw cowboy hat that was several sizes too big because it was his dad's old hat.

Two-year-old Nick didn't want to be left behind. I noticed him crawling through the wire fence with the intention of *helping,* too. He wore his blue overalls and water boots.

As I stood back and watched this scene, I recognized how symbolic and special it was. Del had no idea his little boys were following him. They were intent on doing whatever Dad was doing. The beautiful green field with the mountains in the background, the blue sky, and the water running down the ditch made for a picturesque landscape that I thought would make a beautiful painting. I took a mental snapshot of that moment, framed from my point of view from the green, leafy branches of the big cottonwood tree in our yard.

Oh, how I wish I could paint well…I would love to have this picture hanging on my wall instead of just holding the image in my mind.

Not only were the colors beautiful, but the feeling that entered my heart was even more beautiful. A mix of heritage and tradition, along with love and pride in the future. The next generation was literally walking in the footsteps of their dad.

There have been a handful of moments like this in my life. I remember them because of the emotions I felt, and those emotions rise to the surface every time the images sneak into my consciousness.

Do you have any similar "snapshots" from your life that you will never forget? I hope so. God wants us to have joy and happiness. That image of my adorable little boys and their dad brings me joy every time I think about it.

I remember as a little girl walking out to our small milking barn to be with my dad. He would pick me up and sit me on a milk can so I could watch while he did the evening milking. He kept an old transistor radio out there, and I can still see him dancing around to the music while he put the milking equipment on the Holstein cows. He would sing along to the songs and talk to the cows.

These are other moments I wish I could paint. This is one of the few memories I have of my dad; and one of my happier ones.

Today we have cameras on our phones, so it is easier to capture those moments. I hope you are doing just that, wherever you may be. Whether it is that perfect sunset, that special moment with friends and loved ones, or your favorite pet.

But please don't get so busy looking through the lens of your camera that you forget to see that moment with your heart. It's how we feel inside that makes the moment so special.

May God give us many *snapshots* full of happiness and joy.

Mistaken Identity

I WENT TO AN EMS (Emergency Medical Services) conference held in Provo, Utah. I hadn't been for a few years and was a little nervous about going. But as I walked into the convention center, it felt like I was home. It felt comfortable. And I liked seeing familiar faces. I had a really good time and experience. It was great.

Every morning about 6:30ish, our little group would go down and eat breakfast together. At least those of us who were morning people did.

At breakfast the last morning, I had an older gentleman I didn't know greet me like he was happy to see me. He said hi and asked how I was. It made me feel good. After he walked away, I wondered to myself if he thought I was someone else.

As I was finishing my meal, he walked over to my table and talked to me again. He asked if I was so and so, then realized I wasn't that person he knew. He told me I looked just like this other person. We talked a minute, wondering if we had ever crossed paths and where that might have been. He apologized for bothering me, and I told him don't ever apologize for talking to someone he thought he might know. I was glad he'd said something. We wished each other a good day and parted ways. I really wished I could have been the person he had mistaken me for. It was very evident that she was someone he really liked.

My daughter-in-law Danie attended one of the breakout sessions about pediatric emergencies. I met her afterwards, and this same gentleman was walking out of the class, so I approached him and asked if he was having a good day. He turned to me with tears in his eyes and said not really. This class had brought back the memories from years ago of his young child dying in his arms while there was nothing he could do to help him. His anguish was still so raw and real. I told him I didn't know what to say except my heart goes out to him.

This man affected my life in more ways than he could ever imagine. When he chose to speak to me, he made me feel valued. When he shared his vulnerability with me, my heart connected with his, and I was able to *mourn with those who mourn.*

This experience got me thinking. Am I living my life and treating people in a way that makes them happy to see me? Am I the kind of person people feel like they can talk to? Am I the type of person that if someone I know just happens to see someone else who looks like me, they'll be excited to say hi to them?

Whoever it was this man thought I was, I wish I could thank her. I'm so grateful she is living her life in a way that makes other people happy to see her.

––––––––

Now I want to share a different experience that happened to my husband and father-in-law.

While they were eating dinner at a popular

restaurant in town one day, a gentleman at a nearby table overheard them talking. They noticed he kept giving them dirty looks. They are used to getting funny looks at times because of their cowboy hats, but this gentleman had on a cowboy hat, too. Finally, he walked by their table, and they started talking about cattle and where each was from. He was from a place where we had pastured some cattle during the summer months. He let them know he didn't think much of them because of the way we supposedly didn't take care of our cattle. My father-in-law finally got the details out of this other rancher, and they came to the realization that he thought they were someone else. This revelation changed his whole demeaner and attitude to them. They talked longer, finding they shared common beliefs and practices, and ended on more friendly terms.

This experience has stayed with our family through all these years. Are we being good neighbors? Are we checking our livestock and keeping the fences tight? Are we helpful and mindful of each other?

There are many stories people have shared about their parent or grandparent telling their family to *remember who you are and what you stand for*. I love this thought. Do I come from a perfect family? Absolutely *Not*. Do I come from a good family? *Yes*. Do I want to make them proud of me? Of course. But most of all, I want my Father in Heaven to be proud of the person I am becoming.

While others might mistake us for someone else, God always knows who we really are, and His opinion of us is the only one that matters.

The Christmas Orange

*E*VERY YEAR FOR CHRISTMAS since I can remember, I've received a bag of peanuts with a handful of chocolates and an orange at my church's Christmas party. There was talk of stopping this tradition a few years ago, but thankfully, it still continues. In today's world, it's easy to get each of those things. But when it started, those items were cherished treats. My mother-in-law told me that when she was a little girl, getting an orange was an event. She would keep her orange for days, just enjoying the smell, then when she couldn't wait any longer, she would finally eat it, but not all at once. She would extend it out as long as she could. She was so very grateful to have received her special orange.

When was the last time you were truly grateful to eat an orange? Or a peanut? Have we forgotten how to be grateful for the simple things in our lives?

I'm as guilty as the next person for spending too much money on Christmas presents. Some years it is more than others, but I still could trim it down some. One of my most memorable Christmases was one of the leaner ones. On Christmas Eve, I was putting the last of the presents under the tree and remembered I still needed to sew the doll blankets and nightgowns for Kassie's and Cherilyn's dolls. I had forgotten. So out came the sewing machine, and I did my best without a pattern. The doll clothes wouldn't win a prize, but they worked just fine. The material had been given to me, and I was very grateful. I think it was 2 a.m. before I got to bed that night.

One of my most favorite parts of Christmas is the neighbor gifts. This tradition started about thirty years ago. Since we consider everyone in the valley our neighbor, that's more than just a handful of gifts to buy or make. Instead, it has become a fun tradition to see who can come up with the best gift for the least amount of money, usually around a dollar. We've had everything from packets of hot chocolate mix, to 2-liter pop, to bags of popcorn, to a snowman kit, to ice melt, to brownie mix, to bread, to cheeseballs and crackers, to olives, to matches, to toilet paper—that was the big gift for 2020—and so much more. We have some really creative people who come up with some great sayings, along with their simple gifts.

The point is it doesn't take a lot of money to have a good Christmas. The highlight of Christmas Eve for me is reading about the birth of Baby Jesus in Luke Chapter two, and watching a Christmas movie with my family. I also have to add having a nice family dinner and enjoying my Grandma's Tort for dessert.

What is it about Christmas that has the most meaning for you?

Remember, the greatest event in the world took place in humble circumstances. The birth of our Savior happened in a stable, not a palace. He was wrapped in simple swaddling clothes, not golden robes. And the shepherds were his first visitors, if you don't count the animals in the stable. I picture Mary expressing her gratitude that night for the things she had been blessed with.

As we each celebrate Christmas this year, I hope we look for the small and simple things that have the most meaning in our lives. And as I eat my bag of peanuts, chocolates, and the orange, I'll think of the memories shared by the older generations and remember to be grateful for all the simple things I've been blessed with in my life.

Acts of Service

I HAD A SONG get stuck in my head one day. It's called "Love Helps Those Who Cannot Help Themselves," by Paul Overstreet. It got me thinking about how the way we treat people really does matter.

The song talks about a grandmother who couldn't get out much anymore, but every day, someone would check on her, stop in to see her, or run errands for her. The older we get, the slower we get, that is just a fact of life. We go from doing everything ourselves to needing help or going without.

The song also talks about a farmer who became ill right before planting time. He wasn't able to get his crop in the ground. But someone planted his fields and come fall, he had the best crop he'd ever had.

Are we aware of the people around us? Are we noticing if something is wrong with them and if they need some help? What have we done to help someone lately?

When my mother-in-law was in the hospital and not expected to live much longer, we tried to be there as much as possible with her. It was in the springtime, so, of course, there were animals to be fed and crops to be planted. We have good neighbors and friends who took the time to help feed our animals, along with their own, so we could concentrate on family and plan a funeral. And I'm not talking about just feeding the dogs and a couple of steers.

Funny story: Our close friends offered to help do our chores for the day, even though they aren't ranchers. Chores included feeding several baby calves a bottle and feeding grain and hay to the 4-H steers. Well, I got a phone call from her saying they were having a little bit of trouble. They couldn't get the calves to drink the bottles of milk. I was surprised because those little calves will about run you over try-ing to get to their bottle. Then she told me the gold-colored calf had tried to drink the bottle for a minute, but none of the rest would touch theirs. Then I started to laugh. The bottle calves were all black-hided and weighed between one hundred and two hundred pounds, and the 4-H steers, which included a gold-colored one, weighed around nine hundred to one thousand pounds. They had been trying to feed the 4-H steers bottles of milk. We all had a really good laugh about it. And I still love telling this story.

For some of us, it is really hard to accept help. We are uncomfortable with people doing things for us. We'd much rather be the ones helping others. I've been told that when we refuse someone's offer of help, we deny them the joy of giving. Maybe we could even think of it as our way of helping them by accepting their help. That was a mouthful, but I hope you get the point.

I was raised to help my neighbors, and I grew up watching service in action. One of the times in my young life when this made such an impression on me was when my dad was diagnosed with cancer. For the two years of his surgeries and treatments, then after his death, we had many acts of service and kindness shown to us, which we appreciated so much.

I also watched my mother as she performed acts of kindness and service for others. I will always remember how she bought a cute glass pumpkin cookie jar and filled it with homemade cookies for my elderly piano teacher and her husband. When I gave my teacher the cookie jar, she teared up. Her words to me are seared into my mind and heart. She said, "Your mom just became a widow, and we should be doing things for her, but instead she's doing things for us." My mother taught me a lesson that day that is still with me fifty years later. It doesn't matter what hardships I am going through, there is always something I can do for someone else.

The act of service most of us are familiar with is taking food to a family when there is a death or serious illness. No one really feels like eating, let alone fixing themselves something to eat when there are more serious matters on their minds.

When I worked as a secretary at Thiokol in Northern Utah, my co-worker's dad died. She and her dad were really close, and I wanted to do something for her. The people in my work group chipped in to pay for a meal for her and her family. I bought the food and delivered it. I had also taken time to make a special cake that I knew she liked. No one was home when I arrived, but I dropped off the food and a note, letting her know we cared about her. She told me later that even though she hadn't felt like eating, she had at least eaten a few bites of the cake.

I've also witnessed acts that have left me sobbing. In the agriculture world, the county fair is a big deal. The 4-H and FFA (Future Farmers of America) projects involve lots of work, time, effort, and support. It culminates the week of the fair when the youth show their animals and then sell their animal at the auction on the final day.

During one of my first years of being

involved with the Box Elder County Fair, I witnessed something that affected me deeply. After all these years, some of the details are hard to remember, but I very clearly remember that sale day of the fair. A family had moved into the county and their oldest son wanted to take an animal to the fair. This family hadn't participated in 4-H before, if I remember right, so this was all new.

The boy obtained a lamb and was very diligent in walking it and caring for it. Just before the fair, the young boy was killed in a tragic accident. The fair committee let this boy's lamb still be shown in the fair by his little brother. On sale day, the auctioneers told the crowd just who this lamb belonged to and what had happened to the young boy. Then they started the bidding.

Buyers' hands started raising in the air so fast the men in the auction ring couldn't keep up with all the bids. A winner was finally declared, and everyone cheered for the buyer willing to donate the incredible amount of money to the family. Then something even more incredible happened. The buyer donated the lamb back to be sold again and raised even more money on top of what he was donating. I can still see the parents standing in the auction ring with their young family and the lamb, tears streaming down their faces at the generosity being shown to them. This same lamb was sold several times that day, then gifted back to the family.

I was more proud than ever that day to be a part of the agriculture community. I've been blessed to see this scene repeated several times over the years. Each time, I am brought to tears.

I believe each genuine act of service is recorded in heaven. Big or small, it doesn't matter. It's the intent with which it is offered. God relies on us to be His hands here on earth. He will let us know who needs our help. We just need to be willing, and to listen for the promptings.

I'm sincerely grateful for the service given to me and my family through the years. I feel I fall short in giving service. But instead of being dragged down with guilt, I choose to think instead that this just means I have room for improvement. And I'd be willing to bet we could all do a little better at it.

Service is a powerful way to make a difference.

Inasmuch as ye have done it unto
one of the least of these my brethren,
ye have done it unto me.

— MATTHEW 25:40

Poetry

I HAVE A VERY CLEAR MEMORY of the day when I was a teenager that I found some poems in our filing cabinet. Mom said they were written by my dad. One poem was about a man who had made a date with two different women, one a blonde and one a brunette, for the same dance. That night, he stood up the blonde. After waiting for a time, she went with her parents anyway. Her dad was part of the band. Upon arrival, she saw the young man with the other girl. He had been found out and was caught between the blonde and the brunette. The moral of the story was the guy would just never date another girl with hair.

When I commented about the poem to my

mom, she told me it was true. She was the blonde. So, apparently, she forgave my dad. But she never would tell me who the brunette was. I think I know who it was, though, but I'll never tell.

When I realized that my dad had written a poem about real events, it inspired me. I thought it was really cool that one could write poetry that tells a true story. In my limited life experiences up to that point, poems were usually a little *weird* and written by people who could tell a tall tale. That day was a revelation for me.

It wouldn't be until years later that I would take the time to write my own poems.

I had several opportunities to write poems, some for other people and some just for myself. I've written about courtships, having kids, and funny happenings. My favorite one was when I tried my hand at cowboy poetry. I was stuck in a truck waiting while my husband rode his horse through the cows to check on them. I grabbed a notebook and pen and started writing a poem about the cold wintery day that we had three calves that needed extra attention to stay alive.

Thought I'd share it with you all. Hope you enjoy it.

To Be a Rancher's Wife

It was early one winter mornin'; it had been cold that night.
He'd went out to check the calves in the early morning light.
She hurried through the house as he kicked at the back door.
And as she let him in, he strode on past and laid a new calf
    on the kitchen floor.

"Have ya got some old rugs, Hon? Thisn's purty cold.
Warm a little milk and turn the heat up a bit," she was told.
He'd disappeared out the door, but she heard him kick again.
And she watched as he came bringin' another frozen one in.

"Thisn's the twin sister, and I thought she'd gone to heaven.
Her eyes were glazed over, but just now I noticed she's still a
    breathin'.
We'll have to bathe her, Hon," as he plopped her in the tub,
And he strode on out the door to get yet another scrub.

With the two settled in the kitchen amid old rugs and burlap sacks,
They headed to the tub to their other little task.
They slowly warmed her up, but there was still a little doubt
If this little Hereford calf would ever get thawed out.

After about an hour, the calf was doin' OK,
And they put her with the other two until later on that day.
When he came to take the calves out, he turned and hugged
*   her tight.*
"Thanks for your help, Hon, sorry it made the house look a sight."

After he left to go do chores, she looked at the mess she had.
She'd helped to save three calves, and so she wasn't mad.
It's a good thing she was raised like this, she'd done this all
*   her life.*
And this is what she'd wanted, to be a rancher's wife.

KELLIE KUNZLER
21 Nov 90

We all have something or someone that inspires us to do what we do. My dad inspired me to write poetry. And it happened years after he had died. Did he realize as he wrote his poems that they would affect me like they have? I doubt it. As far as I know, he didn't really share his writings with many people. Oh, how grateful I am he took the time to pen his thoughts and experiences in a creative way.

My dad wrote a Christmas poem that told me a lot about how he felt about our Father in

Heaven. It is a treasure to my family and me. Dad didn't always make it to church every Sunday, but we knew he believed in God.

And I never knew my dad had been in the army until I read one of his poems. Apparently, he'd joined but didn't serve very long, and I was told he was given a medical discharge. I'd only ever known him to be a dairyman, farmer, then a rancher. And my Dad, of course. And he became a deputy sheriff shortly before he died from cancer when I was eight years old. I felt like I'd discovered a treasure trove as I read through his poems.

Even as girl, I liked hearing people talk about the *good old days.* Finding out things about my dad's personal history through his poetry helped change my perception of how to make a record about someone's life. I think this was just another step that led to me getting a degree in family history research.

Would I still have become a writer and a poet, even if my dad wasn't one? Possibly. But I know that what he wrote inspired me to write.

Who has been an inspiration to you?

If they are still alive, take time to let them know how you feel about them. Everyone likes to know they made a difference to someone.

And if while digging in the past
you find a treasure trove,
Tell us all about it in the form of a poem.

Doing Our Part

STAY SAFE. BE SAFE. We hear these words or say them almost every day.

This phrase comes to mind when I sit watching a wildfire burning, and the people I know and love are trying to put it out. What makes them willing to put their lives in danger? The desire to help. Help to save others; from losing what they hold dear. The desire to make a difference in the world.

I know and understand these feelings. The whole reason I get to watch these people fight the fire is because as an AEMT (Advanced Emergency Medical Technician), I help man the ambulance in case someone gets hurt. Why am I willing to do this? The desire to help.

When you live in a rural community, you quickly realize that you need to step up and do your part if you want things to get done, have community gatherings, or have the benefit of a fire department, ambulance service. It takes all of us helping out for these things to happen. The desire to help is a great thing, but without action, that desire is an empty thought.

There are many different ways you can help out. Look around your community, school, or church for a need. I'm thinking you might find more than you realized.

They say the road to Hell is paved with good intentions. That may or may not be true, but I do know this, when Jesus told the parable of the good Samaritan, he was really sharing a story about someone having a desire to help, acting on it, and making a difference in someone's life. The first two people who passed by the man who had been beaten and left for dead either had no desire to help or chose not to act on their desire to help. Thankfully, the Samaritan chose to act.

How many of us would have chosen to act?

Now I'm not saying that everyone needs to be involved in everything, but I urge you to choose something you are passionate about or willing to learn about and to act. Heavenly Father has given us this time on earth to learn and help others. Jesus has shown us by example how to help others. What better way to Be Safe than to choose to follow God's teachings?

The Scriptures are full of examples of people willing to help others. I guess you could also say the Scriptures are full of examples of people who chose not to.

I believe most people have a strong desire to help others and make a difference in the world. It's those who act on those desires who make all the difference.

JK

Focus

MY DAUGHTER, Hope, took a beautiful photo when she went to do her evening chores. We had been blessed with a lot of moisture, and the rain had formed an extra big puddle along the road. She took time to use the reflection of the water to mirror the tall trees and clouds partially obscuring the sun. The shades of blue, gray, and white blended well together. I love that she saw the beauty and wanted to capture it. She came in so excited to show me the pictures she had taken. I loved them.

How we choose to look at things is so important. Hope could have been annoyed she had to deal with puddles and mud to get the grain and feed her calves. Instead, she focused on the beautiful reflection.

What are you choosing to focus on, the annoying parts or the beautiful parts?

When you take a photograph, the camera only *sees* what you are focusing on. You are not going to get a picture of your dog if you point the camera at the cat. You'll end up with a picture of the cat.

If I choose to focus on all the things that annoy me, I'm going to be annoyed all day long. I know this to be true because I've done it. Several times, in fact. I can guarantee you won't have a good day.

They say you attract what you are thinking about or focused on. It's true, as much as we'd like to pretend otherwise.

If you want to have a great day, start looking for all the good things happening in your life. Pay attention to the kindness shown to you throughout the day. Look for ways you can help people. I can safely say that if you do these things, you will be happy throughout your day.

My experience at the county fair one year was just a little bit different than most. I had some health issues, which made me slow down my pace that week. And while I recognized there were things that were affecting people negatively, I chose to put my focus on the positive things going on around me. I looked for the ways people were helping each other.

I saw kids cleaning up dirty stalls that didn't even belong to their animals. I saw kids encouraging each other before they went into the show ring. I saw siblings helping siblings with their animals, and parents and others step in to help when an animal didn't want to be in the show ring. I saw a judge take time to teach and help the kids. I saw many people helping tend the little ones of overwhelmed parents. I saw people getting the head of a steer (that didn't belong to any of their children,) unstuck from a panel. I saw people bidding on animals belonging to kids they didn't even know. I saw kids wanting to donate their 4-H animal check to worthy causes to help other people. I saw people sharing their fair food. I saw people climbing down under the bleachers to retrieve fallen objects for others. I saw people giving their *rodeo crowd prizes* to younger kids who weren't lucky enough to catch a frisbee, toy, or t-shirt. I saw someone find a $20 bill and try to track down the owner. I saw people be excited for others when they did well with their exhibits. I saw people make room so others could sit by them. I saw friendships renewed.

And I saw Gratitude. Like the mother grateful her daughter's phone had been found and returned. Like the parents grateful for the help in finding their *lost* child. And like all the people who were the recipient of the kind of acts I named above.

Interestingly enough, not everyone chose to see those things, even though they attended the same county fair I did. Visiting with friends afterward, they commented on some of the drama and negative things they had witnessed. They had a very different experience than I did.

I was not oblivious to those other things. I just consciously made the choice to not focus on them.

The apostle Paul encourages us to look for ". . . whatsoever things are lovely, whatsoever things are of good report; if there be any virtue, and if there be any praise, think on these things." (Philippians 4:8)

Good advice.

Sometimes it can be hard to see the good. But we get to choose. Don't ignore the mud but take the time to see the beauty that comes with it.

JK

Motherhood

MOTHERS EVERYWHERE should be acknowledged and appreciated. It's not easy being a mother. My road to becoming a mother involved infertility, miscarriages, and lots of prayers and tears. Then my journey through motherhood has involved ups and downs, joy and frustrations, along with more prayers and tears. And I wouldn't trade any of it for the world.

I had a friend tell me once that she didn't like Mother's Day because it made her think about how inadequate she was as a mother. I'll admit I've had those feelings, too. When my kids were little, getting everyone ready and to church in one piece didn't necessarily mean I was a great mom. Usually, it involved me yelling or threatening them to not get dirty, bug each other, or spill the Cheerios. Then I felt guilty as I sat through church listening to how we can be more like Jesus. I'm pretty sure Jesus wouldn't have given my kids the look as the container of Cheerios fell and scattered cereal for three rows behind us, then told them they better pick up every single one or else.

One of the most memorable moments of my motherhood took place in the grocery store. When you live as far away from town as I do, you stock up on groceries when you go. You also take all five kids with you in the store and try to keep them focused on the task at hand, all while repeating, "No, we don't need that," as they keep trying to put their favorite treats in the cart. One day in particular, the boys were helping push the second cart behind me when I heard a crash. I turned around to see they had tipped the cart over somehow. Thank goodness we hadn't hit the milk aisle yet, and I had the baby and the two-year-old in my cart. At this point, I was embarrassed, and I'm pretty sure I spoke some words to the effect that they better pick it all up and it better not happen again or else. Have you ever noticed we never define exactly what *or else* is. We just let their imaginations run wild; and what they think of is usually worse than the real thing.

I know I'm not the only mother who has stories to tell. I know of one incident where two little boys were a handful for their mother, especially in the grocery store. They could be very mischievous. There was one time, though, that they got away from their mother and noticed a bottle of pickles already broken in the aisle. They thought it would be funny to pretend that they'd broken it. When their mother found them, she assumed they'd done it, and they were in big trouble. I'm pretty sure we've all assumed things based on prior behavior. Plus, they pretended it was them. The two boys grew up to be good men who I think a lot of. And Gina, you are a saint…

On one occasion I worked hard to convince my neighbor, Debbie, that our kids would be fine playing while we visited and watched a show. She was a little hesitant, but finally relented. When we finally checked on the kids, I realized she had a right to be nervous. Her boys had decided it would be fun to make their own bubbles and had poured dish soap all over their bunkbed. I learned that a mother's intuition is particular to our own children and should *not* be ignored.

Then we have those times our kids behave and are kind and thoughtful, and we forget all the ways they frustrate us. I've learned that if I will try and do my best as a mom, however inadequate that is, God will help me. I just have to remember to trust Him and His timing.

When I was finally able to become a mother, I realized there are so many women who wish they could be one. And I want you to know that I see you. I see how you love my kids. I see how you love your nieces and nephews. I see how you love the kids you teach. I see your acts of kindness. I see the difference you make in others' lives and the joy you bring to the world. I see you. But most importantly, God sees you.

So, I hope everyone can find some happiness in knowing that you really do make a difference to someone.

I wrote this poem after an especially trying day as a mother. All the following events really happened. I hope you get a good laugh out of it. I *finally* did.

End of Mom's Rope

"I've had it," I said. My husband raised his brow.
"Everyone to bed. Get your pajamas on right now."
"But Mom, it's only 6:30. You're not being very fair."
"Well, I'm the Mom," I said, "and I don't really care."

"Havin' a good day, Hon?" said my husband with a grin.
"Nope, and don't you argue cuz right now you wouldn't win."
We heard all five kids grumble as they headed down the hall.
"I've had it with this mess, and every five minutes someone bawls.

How come when I really need their help to clean the house,
You take Will and Nick to help drive truck or move the cows.
The one, three, and four-year-olds don't help me all that much.
If you're gonna take my two best help, just take the whole
    darn bunch."

"Mom, can we watch a movie? We promise we'll be good.
Why don't you go take a bath and read your brand-new book."
My husband quickly says, "That sounds good to me.
Don't worry about the kids, Hon. I'll keep them quiet as can be."

"That sounds good to me," I said. "But could you guys PLEASE
Pick up the living room first and promise not to tease?"
Five heads nodded yes and hurried to do their task
While I grabbed my brand-new book and headed to my bath.

As I'm soaking in the tub, Del peeks through the door.
"Are you doin' better yet, or do you need a half hour more?"
"I'll be out in a minute; I just needed some peace and quiet.
When these five are wound up, it sounds just like a riot."

Del said, "You're the one who wanted little Wranglers running
    around.
Won't they look so cute." I gave him my best frown.
"If I remember right, it took two to get them here.
All that help will come in handy on the ranch in a few years."

"Yes, dear," says my husband, "But until then they're all yours.
I'll take them off your hands when they're old enough to do
    the chores."
Before I can take aim with the washcloth in my hand
He hurries out the door as fast as he can.

But then he cracks the door and says, "Just one more thing.
Hurry up and get out – the baby's diaper really stinks."

KELLIE KUNZLER
30 Nov 2001

Treasures

I LOVE WESTERN ART. I have three Charles M. Russell prints on my wall. *Bronc For Breakfast* and *Camp Cook's Trouble* are my favorites. One was purchased on our honeymoon. And equally special to me are two calendar pictures from Tim Cox. The one titled *Things Could Get Worse* resembles my husband and the dog we had at the time I bought it at our church auction over thirty years ago. The whole valley had fun bidding me up till I paid an enormously large sum for that picture. But I didn't mind a bit. It still hangs on my wall with the homemade frame made out of old barnwood. It's special to me.

Another picture that graces my wall is an oil

painting of mountains done by my son Bradley when he was a Cub Scout. It's really quite good and I love it. My daughter Kassie learned how to watercolor, and for Christmas one year, she painted me a scene from a photograph taken from the front step of the house where I grew up. It brought back memories of my mom and touched my heart.

I really don't have a lot of wall space in my living room area, but it is filled with pictures. Everything that is hanging on my wall is special. I have framed art that was given to me when my mom died and another one when my father-in-law died. The year Nick started riding stock saddle at a few rodeos, I noticed a painting by Clark Kelley Price titled, *The Round Corral*. Guess what Nick gave me for Christmas that year?

A picture of my dad with his deputy badge is also on my wall. His hat sits at an angle on his head, a small smile on his lips, and I can feel his personality through that picture. I have a few photos from my boys' graduations and Eagle Awards. I have the pictures printed off of my girls' graduations, waiting for me to put them in frames. That needs to be my next project.

Something extra special to me was a gift from my sister. It is a window from my grandparents' house in Juniper, Idaho, with photos of their young family and each of their parents, along with letters written to each other right after their marriage. You see, they had eloped without telling anyone, then came back to their regular routine and jobs until they could figure out what to do.

Its meaning to me is priceless.

I also have a painting of Jesus. It was given to me a few years ago. For a long time, I didn't have a picture of Christ hanging on my wall. Mainly because I felt self-conscious about my imperfections and would feel guilty having Jesus *watch* me every day. Funny what our minds come up with. Especially since Jesus already knows what I struggle with. I finally figured out that He is always with me, sharing His strength.

The saying "Home Is Where The Heart Is" reminds me of the scripture "For where your treasure is, there will your heart be also." – Matt. 6:21

You can probably guess where my heart is and what I consider to be a treasure. My wish for you is:

I hope you find your treasures
Are more than works of art
For the things of greatest value
Are those dearest to the heart.

– KELLIE KUNZLER

The Artist's Brush

THERE WAS A COWBOY POETRY gathering happening in northern Utah, and I signed up for
a booth to sell my book.

While I was sitting at my table for those two
days, I noticed an artist with a booth a little
ways down the aisle. He had planned ahead
and sketched a scene on several small canvases.
While he was at the gathering, he would set
the canvases up on a small easel on a table and
paint. I had a perfect view to watch these oil
paintings develop. He finished a buffalo, a sce-
nic mountain stream, and a little Hereford calf
during that time.

It was interesting to watch him paint that
calf. Herefords have a special place in my heart,

even though we raise mostly Black Angus cattle. Herefords were the original cattle on our ranch. Their red/brown bodies with the white faces are very distinctive. We still have a few in our herd, and his painting reminded me of one of our calves.

My daughter and I enjoyed seeing that particular painting take shape. The second day I was there, I walked over to his booth and asked him where the calf painting was and what he was going to charge for it. His response was,

"Oh, I'm not done with that one yet. I didn't like how it was turning out, so I scraped the paint and will work on it again today."

That surprised me. I thought it looked good from where I was sitting.

Later that day, I watched him put that canvas back up and finish painting the little Hereford calf. It had some changes from the day before and was a really nice painting.

Since then, I've pondered his comments. The picture he originally created was a beautiful work of art. But it didn't feel right to him, and he scraped the canvas and started again. He changed a few things and worked on it until it was "perfect."

At first, I compared myself to the artist. There are many things I do, learning from the process and getting better and better with each attempt. I want things I accomplish or create to be "perfect."

Then something even deeper occurred to me. I realized that I feel a little like that painting. God is my creator. And even though I've got some really good qualities, He knows I can be even better. He is smoothing out or removing certain *brushstrokes* so He can apply an even better layer to me. I'm a work in progress.

So, when something in my life is turned upside down and I'm kicked out of my comfort zone, maybe I should take a deep breath and ask the question, "What is God trying to improve in my life?"

We may be okay with the original version of ourselves, but God sees what we can become. He sees the masterpiece He is creating. He alone knows when it's time to apply the final brushstroke and lay the paintbrush down. Trust in God's vision for you.

> *"...For I know the plans I have for you,"*
> *declares the Lord, "plans to prosper*
> *you and not to harm you, plans to*
> *give you hope and a future."*
>
> — JEREMIAH 29:11

My American Dream

I LET MYSELF get talked into participating in a patriotic cowboy poetry contest. This was the first cowboy poetry contest I'd entered. I enjoyed the writing part, when I wasn't stressing. But trying to memorize it was challenging. I don't usually recite my poems from memory. If I give a poem in a program, I tend to still get nervous, so I just read it instead.

Hope had to listen to me practice memorizing the full two-hours we drove to the event that Friday. The contest was the following morning. I forgot to mention that I usually finish writing my poems at the last minute. That way I feel like I've included everything I can to make it just right. So, I had a limited window to get it memorized. Thank goodness the judges ended up allowing us to use our notes. That was a relief.

When the awards were handed out, I placed 4th. That would be more impressive if there had been more than four of us in my division. (insert laugh here) But I'm glad I took that challenge. My world was expanded, I made some new friends, and I received compliments on my poem. I can't ask for more than that.

This poem was written from my heart. I truly believe in these things. I thought maybe some of you could relate to it, too.

My American Dream

Every morning, I wake up to a beautiful mountain view
And start running through the list of all the things we have to do.
There's horses to feed, cows to check, and breakfast for the crew
And what comes next is bound to change, it's always somethin' new.

I'm livin' the dream, the American Dream, this cowboy way of life.
It may not be for everyone, but I'm happy that it's mine.
Some folks choose to live in New York and Boston and the like,
But give me the wide-open spaces and a horse that I can ride.

I've raised good kids in a special place out here in the West.
Where they work beside us, and we strive to do our best
Just like so many others living across the USA,
Who also dare to dream and who work hard every day.

We're different yet the same, with similar hopes and fears,
We love family, God & country, whether hailing a cab or roping
    steers.
I'm grateful for the soldiers who choose to protect
This nation and its people. They deserve our respect.

When we're at the rodeo, and the flag girls come ridin' in,
I still get chills to see Old Glory whippin' in the wind.
And all the cowboy hats come off to cover up their heart
In respect for this great country of which we are a part.

Freedom isn't free, there's those who've paid the price
And I'm forever grateful for their noble sacrifice.
I'm free to choose which path I take, thanks to those who've
    gone before
And fought for the freedom that reaches from shore to shore.

I love this land, and I love my home, there's no place I'd
    rather be.
Whether it's saddling up and moving cattle or watching an
    eagle on the wing.
May God still bless America, and the stars and stripes always wave.
May it ever be the land of the free and the home of the brave.

   – Kellie Kunzler, 14 March 2024

Stumbling

WHILE GOING THROUGH some of my writing files, I came across a poem I'd written in December of 2022. Normally, my poetry involves rhyming and stanzas, but once in a while I just write down what I'm feeling at that time. I'd like to share it with you.

> I stumbled tonight
>
> On my path to becoming more.
>
> But as I ponder
>
> On my actions,
>
> I can see
>
> My growth
>
> And how I'm changing.

I'm making progress
With who I am.
I'm not who
I want to be,
Yet,
But I'm changing
Slowly.

Even though I don't remember exactly what I was going through then, the feelings I wrote down are still applicable to me today. In fact, I was just thinking similar thoughts a few days ago.

I try so hard to get things right. I have learned to think through my choices and recognize what the consequences will be. And I ask myself if I'm okay with those consequences. If I'm not, I try a different approach.

No one likes getting chewed out or yelled at, including me. But I'm pretty sure we all have at some time in our lives. Some more than others.

I quickly figured out that if I'm helping the person fixing the machinery by holding on to the nuts, bolts, and small parts, I better not drop anything. It only took a couple of times of not being able to quickly hand back that little part for me to figure out how to pay better attention. If something did drop in the dirt, I watched it like a hawk and didn't give up till I had it back in my hand as soon as possible. That way I wouldn't get in trouble.

It can get pretty exhausting always trying to plan ahead for every scenario so I'm doing *everything right* and not getting cussed. It's really more of a trauma response. That's a term I learned a few years ago.

I want to share a little secret with you.

No one is perfect. Not me, not you, not anybody. So, we shouldn't be surprised or feel bad when we make mistakes or others do. It's how we react and what we do with those mistakes that determine what kind of person we are becoming.

One of the hardest times for me made the biggest impact on my future. My mother had come to visit and stay with my family. It was a stressful time for me, and my five young children were not listening to me well. I remember getting after them which involved some yelling. I will never forget my mother witnessing that and her words to me. She told me I sounded just like another person, someone who had treated me similarly and made me feel bad. I was hurt and angry that she would compare me to this person. I made sure my children were okay and left them in the care of my mom while I went for a drive. I needed to cool down and think through my behavior.

As much as I didn't want to admit it, my mother was right. Even though I loved my children, I was not acting like it. I had become like that person I had vowed I wouldn't be like. That hurt. A lot.

Did I completely change overnight? Nope, but I did start changing my behavior to be more in line with Christ's teachings. And little by little, I've been able to change for the better.

It took a little time, but I was finally able to express my gratitude for my mother speaking up to me that day. She had the courage to tell me what I needed to hear, which wasn't easy for either of us.

Life can get so discouraging, though, and we start to believe that we'll never conquer our faults. But, in turning to Christ, we can turn our own lives around.

One of my uncles made a big impression on me. As a child, I witnessed him struggle with his addiction to alcohol. He was a very hard-working man but couldn't give up the bottle. One night, he stopped by our house when he was drunk. I was about nine or ten years old, and I remember being shocked and a little scared at his behavior. His teenage son was with him, trying his best to get his dad to leave and go home. My uncle's addiction was a challenge for his wife and kids and had been for a long time. I think we were all convinced he was never going to change.

During the next ten years, though, I witnessed my uncle overcome that addiction and truly change his life. He became one of my favorite uncles. I loved taking my children to visit him. When I think about miracles and changing our lives for the better, I automatically think of my uncle.

Should we ever give up hope that we or a loved one can do better? Please don't. Even when it seems we stumble often, take a moment to see how far you've already come.

I'm not the same person today that I was ten years ago, five years ago, or even one year ago. Am I perfect yet? Not by a long shot. But am I better than I used to be? Yep.

Sharing Hearts and Sunshine

VERY ONCE IN A WHILE, I get asked to substitute teach at our small rural school. Here's a little secret. I kind of enjoy it. I spent two days in the *little* room with kindergarten thru second graders, all nine of them. Having multiple grades in one room might seem odd, unless you live in a small town, but I'm used to it.

While growing up, I attended a one-room school that went up to sixth grade. I even got to sit in the old-fashioned desks that were hooked together. I thought they were cool. So, teaching four grades at a time is challenging, but doable, especially since we are blessed with some wonderful aides.

I know all twenty-five kids in our school by name. Heck, one's my daughter and most of the others are related somehow. But it still touches my heart when they seek me out to do things with them.

Once while substitute teaching, one of the girls brought me some playdough heart cookies during creative playtime. The next thing I know, she brought half the entire playdough collection to my table wanting me to play with her. Usually, I just sit back and watch, but that day, I chose to play. I rolled the pink dough into a long thin rope and fashioned a heart. This little girl saw what I did and made a blue heart that fit inside my pink one. I loved it. I had to snap a picture. She asked me to send the picture to her mom, too.

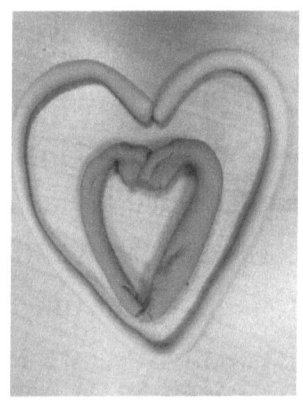

What makes this extra special to me is that this little girl was very shy around me for the first few months of school. I feel lucky that she now talks to me freely and includes me in her world.

Why am I sharing this?

I guess because this little girl made a difference in my life that day, and I like to think I made a difference in hers. I won't forget how it felt to "share my heart" with her.

There is also a young student on my bus route who is always smiling and happy. Some days she will sing the whole way to school or the whole way home. I love it. She usually sits in the front of the bus, so I get to hear her beautiful little voice singing songs about sunshine. How can you not have a good day after being serenaded like that.

We all have the power within us to brighten someone's day, no matter our age. I hope you'll choose to do just that. It can be as simple as sharing a playdough heart cookie or a smile and a song. Remember, one little act of kindness can make a huge impact.

JK

The Golden Rule

I LOVE WHERE I LIVE.
This valley has a beautiful mountain range with several beautiful canyons. Meadows run along the side of and below the highway, mixed amongst the sagebrush and cedar trees. I can hear the birds singing every morning before the sun comes up. I love watching the hawks and eagles ride the air currents, circling above, looking like they are just content to float there for a while. Mama cows graze while their calves follow along, exploring their new world and playing with the other calves. Horse colts test out their new legs, dashing here and there, but never far from their mothers.

I love where I live.

The people here are a great mix of being independent and unified at the same time. We all have the mentality that we take care of our own but will drop whatever we're doing to help someone in need. Self-reliant, but not self-ish. Not perfect, but each of us striving to be the best person we can be.

I love where I live.

We usually celebrate with each other special events, whether a wedding, graduation, or new baby. We also mourn with each other over each loss, big or small. A card, a plate of brownies, a flower, or an offer to help brand, haul hay, or move cattle lets others know we are thinking of each other, and that we care.

Do you love where you live?

Have you heard of the Golden Rule?

"Therefore, all things whatsoever ye would that men should do to you, do ye even so to them." Matthew 7:12

Another way to say this is: Treat others how you want to be treated.

If you want good neighbors, be a good neighbor. If you want respect, show respect. We can all do better at being better. Be the friend you would like to have. You have more influence than you know.

When my daughter Cherilyn moved into town to her own place, I prayed she'd be safe. Remember I'm her mom, and she grew up in a very rural area. Right off the bat, the couple next door introduced themselves and checked in with her, even sharing produce from their garden. The neighbors across the street left her some brownies and a note with their phone number if she needed anything. And her landlords always take care of her lawn. These good people have watched out for her and treated her like a daughter or granddaughter. She cares about them, too.

Those simple acts of kindness have made a lasting impression on our family.

I challenge you to try an experiment. Choose one person to do something kind for. If you want to do it anonymously, that's okay. Then watch what happens. I hope it brings a smile to both of you.

Sometimes, we might not see much of a

difference in the attitude of the receiver. Don't get discouraged. No act of kindness goes unnoticed by God.

The Golden Rule is a good motto to live by. How we treat others really matters. We can make a real difference in each other's lives by practicing kindness and respect.

And if need be, be the one willing to make the first move, and I dare say you'll end up loving where you live, too.

Passing It On

I LIKE TO GO FOR A DRIVE through the ceme-tery on the evening of Memorial Day. The decorated graves testify that these people are remembered and loved.

For thirty-six years, my mother put red roses on my dad's grave. Now my sisters and I carry on that tradition, making sure to put red roses on both of their graves.

My whole life I've spent Memorial Weekend decorating the graves of my ancestors and loved ones.

My family, the aunts, uncles, and cousins, would meet at the cemetery, usually on that Monday morning. We would visit and catch up on the happenings in our families and put flowers on the graves. I loved hearing them tell stories of the people whose graves we were decorating.

Our family always made sure the grave sites were clean from rocks and weeds. When you live in the desert, you don't worry about growing grass in the cemetery. These small communities usually just have sagebrush, crested wheat, and cedar trees. This makes for a nice place for a final resting spot. Each May, Park Valley has a community cemetery clean-up. Trash is picked up and the native grasses are mowed.

As a kid, my 4-H club decided we would clean part of the cemetery that had been neglected and overrun with bushes. As we worked to cut back the thick shrubbery, we discovered some smaller headstones of a couple of the men who had helped settle the Almo Valley. We were so excited. We felt like we had struck gold. For the remaining years I lived in Almo, we made sure those men's graves were taken care of.

In our small community of Park Valley, there are two bachelor brothers who are buried next to each other. One came home from the war years ago and struggled with life. No one had heard of PTSD back then. Even though he struggled, he was always nice to my husband's family. The brothers ran a fix-it shop and did odd jobs for people. My sister-in-law has fond memories of those brothers because her dad would send her on errands to their shop to get things fixed.

The brother that struggled with PTSD eventually took his own life. Every year, my sister-in-law and our family put flowers on their graves. They did not have any posterity, but our family knows their stories, and we remember the good people they were. My children love hearing those stories and make sure we have enough flowers for those brothers.

There is also a spot in our cemetery where a young Indian boy is buried. The story goes that his tribe was traveling through this area and he died unexpectedly. They buried him and his horse here. It has become a tradition that the youth take the time to clean the young boy's grave and decorate it. My children have all been a part of that service, and even though they have grown, they still check that it is being taken care of.

Years ago, I remember hearing a story about a young man who took it upon himself to clean and care for the grave of another young man who had died far from his home in the United States while serving a church mission across the sea. I'm sure this missionary's family thought about him and worried about his unattended grave but flying to another country every year for Memorial Weekend would be expensive. I know they were grateful to that young man for his act of service to their loved one.

I have family members' graves spread throughout many different cemeteries that are hard to travel to. I hit as many as I can. My sisters and cousins do the same. Here in Park Valley, I can care for those graves whose families live far away. And I hope someone will do the same for those places we aren't able to visit.

It's so important for us to remember those who've went before us. Remember their stories. Remember their sacrifices for our country. Remember their kindnesses. And if those memories are not pleasant ones, that is worth remembering, too, so that we can learn from them and become better people.

I remember the red roses and what they represent to our family, love and devotion. We remember the kindness of two bachelor brothers.

That's what I want to pass on to my posterity.

Angels on Earth

I'M VERY GRATEFUL for those people who try to live good lives and listen to the promptings of the Holy Spirit.

There have been many people who I think of as angels on this earth. They have acted on promptings and called me on the phone or shown up on my doorstep when I needed someone to talk to.

One of my friends knocked on my door the day after I had a hurtful experience and didn't know what to do about it. Her genuine care and concern for me helped me share what had happened. I'd acted on an answer to prayer, but it was not what the other person had wanted to hear. They said I wasn't welcome in their home.

I love that person, and it hurt a lot. I needed someone to talk to, and it was no coincidence my friend felt like she needed to visit me that day. I know God sent her to be my earthly angel. And though it took months, that person whom I love reached out to end the rift in our relationship. I knew I had followed the direction of the Spirit, and things eventually turned out good. Having my friend to lean on through that time made a huge difference.

A very dear friend who faithfully attends church felt the need to go home early one weekend. It was a Sunday I was struggling with feelings of self-doubt and the news that one of my friends didn't have long to live. This sister in Christ saw me and sat and talked with me outside our church services. We cried together, and she lifted me up with her loving and caring heart. She is truly an earthly angel.

When we get that thought to give someone a call, stop by someone's home, or make extra treats, do it. God will answer someone else's prayers through you.

Another example of an earthly angel was when

I received a wonderful surprise in the mail. It was a touching, encouraging card from one of my fellow author friends from another state who I stay in touch with. She had been prompted to send me some encouragement. I was humbled and grateful for her words and thoughtfulness. And her confidence in me helped me stay focused as I worked on this book.

A few years ago, I had an experience that taught me the importance of acting on promptings immediately.

In our valley, when someone has their first baby, we have a baby shower and invite everyone. But with each new birth, usually gifts are given anyway as a *congratulations*. A young mother, new to the valley, had a newborn daughter, and a baby shower had been planned a few weeks later. I had my gift ready. As I was leaving for an activity, I felt a strong impression to take the baby gift that day and give it to her. I rationalized that if I gave it to her now, I wouldn't have a gift for the shower. But the impression was so strong that I fixed the gift in a pretty bag, and when I saw her at the activity,

I gave her the present. One week later, she told me they were moving in a couple of days. It had happened rather quickly, and we didn't get to give her the shower.

How glad I was that I had actually listened and followed that prompting. I think God wanted that young mother to know someone cared about her, and I needed the practice of acting on a prompting.

Most of the times we feel that nudge to do something, we might not find out why until much later. This was a rather quick answer to my question.

You don't have to be an important person in the eyes of the world to make a difference in the life of someone. God will work with any-one willing to hear Him. I am blessed to know people who listen and act when He asks.

I guess you could say I'm surrounded by Angels, both those in heaven and those on earth. And oh, how grateful I am for both.

Regret

REGRET IS AN EMOTION that seems to plague a lot of us. I know it does me.

As hard as we try, we don't always do the right thing. Looking back at my life, I wish I'd have done some things differently.

I regret that I joined in the teasing of a boy in my junior high class. The teasing wasn't a fun, good-natured ribbing. I knew better. I knew what it felt like to be picked on. I knew the hurt of not being accepted. I gave in to peer pressure because I was scared that if I didn't join in, the kids would turn on me and start picking on me instead. From the moment I joined in, I knew it was wrong and tried to inconspicuously quit. Not only do I regret joining in, but I also regret not standing up to the crowd.

I regret not finding a way to train a horse. I was in my mid-teens, when I finally bought my very own horse, and she was pregnant. My mare foaled and gave me a little filly. I dreamed of training that little filly. As a yearling, she had been turned out with the other horses on the mountain to graze for the summer. One day we rode out to check on them, and I noticed my filly was missing part of her hoof. We never knew exactly what happened, but there went my dream of training my very own horse. And though I still had the desire, I didn't have the courage and drive to make my dream a reality through other means.

I had a fairly close relationship with my mother. She was widowed at age thirty-eight, so we kids were everything to her. She loved her family and knew what was going on with all four of her children and the grandkids, too. We talked at least once a day, and sometimes twice. When you talk that often with someone, sometimes the conversation doesn't last that long. It doesn't have to. She was a listening ear and a wise giver-of-advice.

One afternoon, she phoned me about the time I should have been starting supper for my family. I was sitting in our office trying to have a conversation with Mom and my kids kept interrupting me. I was getting so frustrated with them and decided I had better go fix dinner. I could tell Mom still wanted to talk, but I told her, "I gotta go. I'll call you later."

Well, I got busy and tired and never called her back.

The next morning, I had the first opportunity I'd had in literally a few years, to ride with my husband to the livestock sale in Burley, Idaho. I was excited and wanted to call Mom to see if she was going to be in town so we could go to lunch together. My husband, one-year-old daughter, and I started for town, and I called Mom on my cell phone. I was surprised when my brother, who lived on the ranch near her, answered instead of Mom. When I asked to speak with Mom, he told me she was gone. I thought he meant she had either left for town or that he was teasing me. Then he said he'd just found her body. She had died the night before.

To this day, I regret not finishing the conversation, cutting her off, and not calling her back.

If you could go back in time, are there things you wish you could change?

I believe that the experiences we have in life help shape who we are and what we learn to do.

During a trip to the National Finals Rodeo in Las Vegas, Nevada, I had a conversation with a very wise and special teenage girl. Molly and her brother are friends with my kids and came with us on that trip. When Molly spoke to her siblings on the phone, I noticed she ended each conversation by telling them she loved them. I was so impressed that a teenager was unashamed to say that. When I commented about it to her, she shared a story with me.

There had been a time when she and her brothers had been fighting and when the boys left, they were still mad at each other. Later that day, there was an accident, and her brothers were hurt and taken to the hospital. The thought that the last words she had said to them were full of anger filled her with regret.

She vowed that day to never part ways angry nor let a chance go by to tell her family and friends that she loved them.

What a great example to all of us. Molly didn't just think about changing her behavior, she did. She learned from her regrets.

Having my mom die unexpectedly opened my eyes to all the times I had missed out by not going to family get-togethers and spending time with them. My husband, Del, doesn't really like socializing, so having work to do on the ranch would take priority. And when we would go, it was usually for about an hour, then we'd have to head home.

Now, when my sisters or Del's sisters want to get together, I try really hard to get there, even if I have to go alone. My daughters usually make it. Sometimes my husband and sons do, too. I count myself lucky when that happens.

Whenever I talk to my kids, I try to tell them that I love them. Some of my adult kids think I'm a little weird when I do. But some of them will say it back or even initiate it. I'm hoping for a one hundred percent one day. Our youngest, Hope, is still living with me, so she hears it all the time. I love it when she says it to me first.

One of the best examples in the Scriptures of changing our behavior is Paul, formerly known as Saul. He had been persecuting Christians in the worst possible way. Then, he had an amazing experience while traveling to Damascus which caused him to see life in a new way. His name was changed, and he became one of the apostles of Jesus Christ. He had many regrets and chose to stop that behavior and change how he lived his life.

Our lives don't have to be full of regrets. If we choose to learn from them as they happen, we change the direction of our journey. We realize that what we did is not something we want to do again. Then, like Paul, we take the steps to change how we live.

Oddly enough, our regrets can become some of our greatest blessings.

A Generational Thing

WHILE STUDYING for my bachelor's degree, I had a class assignment to take photos of what my life was like. I wasn't sure where to begin. I couldn't use old photos, they had to be new that week. I ended up taking photos of my school bus, a tractor loading hay, feeding the cows in the old ranch truck, my husband, Del, and daughter-in-law, Danie, being lifted up on the backhoe to check the levels in the syrup tank for the cows. Don't worry, they were safe and didn't fall in the tank or off the loader.

I realized I had spent much of my time behind the wheel of bigger vehicles, not just a car. I actually don't mind driving. It provides me a freedom I wouldn't otherwise have. It's also something I have in common with my parents and grandparents. I first learned to drive behind the wheel of a feed truck, which sometimes included the two-ton truck. In fact, when I took driver's ed, the instructor told me he knew I already knew how to drive and didn't bother testing me on some of the skills. I've driven a truck during beet harvest, the swather, many tractors, and the school bus.

My mom learned to drive by helping her dad on their dry farm in Juniper, Idaho. I have a picture of her in the driver's seat of the two-ton truck with a smile on her face. My dad and mom drove the milk truck route to Park Valley, Utah, and back to Malta, Idaho, to the Kraft factory. This was over one hundred miles round trip. Then they started driving the school bus route from Almo, Idaho, to Malta and back. Dad took the job initially, and Mom was the one who ended up driving the route. She drove school bus for over forty years before health issues forced her to retire.

My kids all grew up driving on the ranch. And my sons have their own semis and started a trucking company hauling livestock. They kind of enjoy being behind the wheel of those big rigs. I guess you could say driving big vehicles is a generational thing.

Isn't it funny how some things seem to just be part of your family? Agriculture is a big part of my life and has been in my family line for generations. God willing, it will be for many more.

What is something that has been part of your family for generations? A talent for music? Construction? Law enforcement? Community service? Teaching?

I've a neighbor who is a third-generation teacher. She's great at it, and my children loved having her for their teacher. Her dad eventually became a principal, and she did the same. Her daughter is following in her footsteps and working on her own teaching degree. I know the daughter will do a great job, too.

I realize not every kid will end up doing the same thing as their parents. And sometimes that is a good thing. But I'll admit it makes me happy to see those that want to keep the family's legacy going. Especially with farming and ranching. There is a special feeling you get when you watch your little boy put on his dad's old beat-up cowboy hat and follow him around the corrals. And it seems in the blink of an eye they are the one fixing that old tractor, putting up the hay, and riding the colts. As a parent, it makes me happy that my kids love the same things I do.

Another thing that I can claim has been passed down through my family line is a firm belief in God. I don't come from a family of perfect people by any means. I have had good examples to follow and a few examples of what not to do. But I know who I can turn to when hard times come. And I know who to thank for my blessings.

No matter what your occupation is, my hope is that you will carry on those things that hold a special place in your family. Maybe you can improve on them or even start some new traditions of your own. As long as it's something you love. And God willing, you'll be able to pass them on to many more generations to come.

Small Things

I'VE OFTEN HEARD THE QUOTE, "By small and simple things are great things brought to pass." I didn't quite know what to think about that during my teenage years. The older I've gotten, the more it makes sense.

A really good example is that a boat is steered by a very small rudder. It doesn't matter the size of the boat. The rudder is always smaller. It is also a very vital part of getting the boat to its final destination. I don't know a lot about boats. In fact, I can count on one hand the number of times I've been on a boat. But I thought this was a really cool analogy.

This made me think of something my friend Michele shared with me.

When she took an Emergency Medical Technician (EMT) course many years ago, the instructor made her feel like she was the smartest person he'd ever met. When she told him that, his response was, "You are." His words were life-changing for a woman who'd struggled doing schoolwork and had flunked out of college three times. They didn't talk about ADHD back then. Michele passed the EMT test the first time she took it. Having her instructor, Cole, believe in her gave her the courage to keep learning. Those two little words from an EMT instructor have led to Michele getting a medical degree. Don't underestimate the power of your words.

I was visiting with some of my kids about things that have made a difference in our lives. My son, Bradley, shared that as a little kid, getting to ride in my cousin Hank's semi-truck when he hauled our cattle was the greatest thing ever. He's had a love of ranching and semis and now owns his own. He loves driving truck and started a trucking company with his brothers. He is loving it. Brad watched his buddy give some very excited little boys a ride in his semi, and it brought back those feelings he had as a little boy and the joy it brought him. He's living his dream.

When Hank gave Bradley and his brothers a ride that day, it was just a small thing to him but had a huge impact on my boys.

My oldest son, Will, also told me that getting to go all the time with his grandpa and dad as they worked on the ranch gave him a love for the cowboy life. Today, Will's pretty handy on a horse or a tractor and is usually the one fixing the equipment. He said having them trust him to do chores and different jobs really meant a lot to him. And getting to hear Grandpa Dee's stories about cowboying in the old days was icing on the cake.

I sent Will out most days to *work* with Dad and Grandpa, and he felt valued and wanted to be a cowboy just like them. What an impact it made on Will that they took the time to have him tag along.

When my daughter, Cherilyn, was in grade school, she was asked what she wanted to be when she grew up. She didn't know, but one of the other kids wanted to be a veterinarian. That got her thinking. A few years later, her brother, Nick, asked Cherilyn if she wanted to come with him to take his mare to the vet. It had somehow gotten a fence post shoved through its flank. The vet that treated the horse took the time to explain everything he was doing. When the college classes offered in high school included a veterinarian technician, Cherilyn jumped at the chance.

Someone who shared their own dream and a vet who took the time to teach and answer questions inspired Cherilyn. Now she has a career that she loves, and she is good at it.

I have an uncle who gives me a hug every time he sees me. For a girl whose dad died when she was eight, his hugs mean the world to me. I feel loved and cared for each time. I don't think he knows how much that small act has affected me all these years. Thank you, Uncle Ted.

These stories I've shared all have one thing in common. Not one of those people who had a big impact on others set out to change someone's life by their actions. They were just doing normal things. Imagine what we could do for the world if we were intentional in being kind and helping others.

I believe there are no coincidences. We are meant to meet certain people. Either they will make an impression on us, or we will affect them somehow. I don't know that I would have believed that fully just a few years ago, but I do now. Wherever we are, what we do matters.

And it is the little things that make the biggest impact.

The Difference

ETTING A HORSE to trust you is a big part of the training process. Horses' personalities are as varied as people are. Some catch on quickly and will quit fighting you. Others challenge even the best horse trainers. On our ranch, the day we halter and tie up the yearling colts for the first time can get pretty interesting. My daughter-in-law, Danie, has a mare whose colts always seem to be very hard-headed. They watch those colts closely to make sure they don't hurt themselves. I've often thought if the colts would just realize we weren't going to hurt them, we just want to teach them the things they need to learn, maybe they would cooperate better.

I follow a horse trainer on social media. He weaves messages about God into each video he shares. He shared a story of one horse that wouldn't calm down and was determined to find a way to escape the round pen where this trainer was trying to work with it. The man found himself asking the horse why it wouldn't just calm down, stop running, and trust him enough to come to him. All the trainer wanted to do was show the horse what he was capable of, to help it reach its full potential. Then he realized that those words that were coming to him to speak were as if God was talking to him personally. It was a message he needed. And as I watched the video, it was like God was saying the same things to me, asking those same questions. The impression was so strong for me that I took time to write them down and ponder them.

A horse being trained to allow a rider on it is just like God asking us to allow Him to teach us and take the reins from us. God's asking us to trust that His way is the better way for our lives. We don't have to fight Him. God is patiently waiting for us to quit running and come to Him.

God can help us in ways too numerous to count. We can receive inspiration from many sources. I'm so grateful when God gives me those "Ah ha" moments.

What has made the biggest difference in my life?

Making the choice to follow Jesus Christ and do His will instead of mine. When I struggle to live life on my own terms, I realize I'm missing something.

When I faced some life-changing decisions later in my life, I realized that what I wanted didn't really matter when it came right down to it. I had felt peace in the past when I turned to God for answers. And I knew I needed help to make the right decisions in this instance.

I committed at that time to seek God's will over my own. As hard as it was to follow and act on the answers I was receiving, I did. Did it turn out how I had hoped? No. But I have no doubt that things turned out the way they were supposed to. There is peace in that knowledge.

Since that time, I have had more opportunities to practice this.

In my first book, I shared the story of how I went back to college and graduated with a bachelor's degree. God asked me to go back to school and get a degree in family history research. When I finally quit trying to talk Him out of it by saying how busy I was, I promised I would do it if He would prepare a way. Two months later, things changed, and I had the time. So, I spent the next three and a half years taking online courses. I've been blessed with friendships and greater knowledge because of this. And I'm waiting patiently on the promptings of how to utilize that knowledge. Okay, kind of patiently waiting.

The second part to that is after graduating, I was again asked to step out of my comfort zone and publish a book. By this point, I recognized this was something God wanted me to do, even if I was nervous about it. I have learned so much through this process. Not only about the publishing process, but about myself and how to hear Him.

Letting God direct my life is something I have had to work at. I'm still very human and tend to not clue in sometimes to those promptings. But He is patient with me. And I love the peace that comes from following Him and letting Him guide me.

There are times I catch myself trying to tell God how things should be happening. The funny part is that I forget that He knows everything better than I do. I've learned to laugh at myself when I realize when I'm doing it. I picture God shaking His head and smiling down at me while He waits patiently for me to clue in that I'm lecturing Him, *again.*

There is a saying: If we turn our life over to God, He will do more with it than we ever could.

I've finally started to believe it; and that has made all the difference.

Acknowledgements

THANK YOU to my family for letting me share our lives with all of you. I know you'd all rather be quietly working in the background instead of being in the spotlight. You mean everything to me. *Del, Will, Danie, Callie, Nick, Bradley, Emily, Kassie, Cherilyn, and Hope.

Thank you to my friends at Author Ready. Your continued support and encouragement mean so much to me.

A huge hug and thank you to my family, friends, and neighbors who have supported me in my writing and are continually cheering me on.

And I'm grateful to God for putting these thoughts in my heart and asking me to share them with you all. Rarely does He ask us to do easy things, but He does help us every step of the way.

About the Author

KELLIE KUNZLER was raised on a ranch in the little town of Almo in Southern Idaho. She grew up helping on the ranch and singing in her family's country western dance band. Her love of reading started at a young age and opened up a whole new world to her beyond the mountain valley where she lived.

After graduating from college to be a secretary, she met and married her cowboy, Del Dee. Kellie and Del have six children and continue the tradition of raising cattle and horses in Rosette, on their sixth-generation ranch in Northern Utah.

Kellie recently earned a bachelor's degree while studying family history research. She plays the organ and piano for her church congregation, is an AEMT on the ambulance service, and is a 4-H leader. She also drives a school bus for the local school in Park Valley. Kellie spends most of her time writing, helping out on the ranch, and being a wife, mother, and grandmother.

JK

www.ingramcontent.com/pod-product-compliance
Lightning Source LLC
Chambersburg PA
CBHW021116130626
46554CB00002B/721

9798894540245